TELEPATHOLOGIES

Cortney Lamar Charleston

saturnalia books

Distributed by University Press of New England
Hanover and London

Saturnalia Books
105 Woodside Rd.
Ardmore, PA 19003
info@saturnaliabooks.com

ISBN: 978-0-9980534-4-8
Library of Congress Control Number: 2016952338

Book Design by Saturnalia Books
Printing by McNaughton & Gunn
Cover Art: The New Age of Slavery by Patrick Campbell

Author Photo: Ayasha Guerin

Distributed by:
University Press of New England
1 Court Street
Lebanon, NH 03766
800-421-1561

This collection was an immense undertaking for many reasons, something that required the best of me in the worst of times. I wouldn't have been able to pull it off without the love and support from a mighty few, and to them I owe thanks. Thank you, Lord, for letting me live to write this. Thank you Ruani, for going through the storm with me, always, and always coming out the other side. Thank you to my parents, Pamela and Vincent, for always believing in me and instilling in me willingness to trust the steadiness of my own mind and the callings of my heart. Thank you to my brother, Cameron, and my sisters, Camille and Calah, for your unwavering love. Thank you to my grandparents, Joan and George and Margie and Gomez, thank you to all my aunties and uncles and cousins who keep me grounded in the past, the present and the future. Thank you to my high school and college friends for always having my back over the years no matter how long it's been—Ed, Lauren, Tillus, Geoff, Julius, Sylvia, Glenn. Thank you for pushing me to be bold, Victoria. Thank you for listening, Caroline. Thank you for encouraging to get these words out there, Josh. Thank you, Carlos. Thank you, Warren. Thank you to my whole Excelano Family for existing and inspiring me to pick up a pen in the first place. Thank you, José: I see you brother! Thank you, Nate: I see you brother! Thank you, Nabila: I see you sister! Thank you, Aziza: I see you, sister! Thank you to The Conversation and the folks I'm in conversation with. Thank you to Cave Canem for making ways for me and us. Thank you, Henry, thank you, Chris, thank you, Saturnalia! Thank you, Doug. Thank you, Evie. Thank you to everyone who reads this note. Forever.

Several poems in *Telepathologies* have previously appeared in print and online publications, sometimes in slightly different versions. My sincere thanks goes to the following publications for generously giving first homes to the work in this collection:

Apogee, Beecher's Magazine, Beloit Poetry Journal, Blunderbuss Magazine, Chiron Review, Connotation Press: An Online Artifact, Contraposition Magazine, CURA: A Literary Magazine of Art & Action, Drunk in a Midnight Choir, Eleven Eleven, ep;phany, FOLIO, Fourteen Hills, Fugue, Hayden's Ferry Review, HEArt Online: Human Equity Through Art, Huizache: The Magazine of Latino Literature, IDK Magazine!, J Journal, The Journal, Juked, Kweli, Matter: A Journal of Political Poetry & Commentary, The Missouri Review, Mobius: The Journal of Social Change, Nashville Review, The Offing, One Throne Magazine, Passages North, Pleiades, pluck! The Journal of Affrilachian Arts & Culture, Puerto del Sol, Radius, Rattle, RipRap Journal, River Styx, Rogue Agent, The Rumpus, Southern Humanities Review, THRUSH Poetry Journal, Toe Good Poetry, Up the Staircase Quarterly, Waxwing, Winter Tangerine Review

Additionally, "A Boogie Night, Age 12" appeared in the inaugural edition of *Independent Best American Poetry*.

"How Do You Raise a Black Child?" was adapted to film by Seyi Peter-Thomas in collaboration with Motionpoems, a non-profit organization based in Minneapolis, MN dedicated to integrating verse and visual art. The film is part of Motionpoems' seventh season, which showcases the work of Cave Canem poets.

TABLE OF CONTENTS

TELEPATHOLOGY
[tel-uh-puh-thol-*uh*-jee]

noun, plural – telepathologies

---

1. A subliminally transmitted belief espousing the sub-humanity of certain groups of people and deviating from healthy emotional and social cognition.

    a. *Media*: The argument of sub-humanity levied at specific populations through the selective presentation of negative images or the use of coded language.

HOW DO YOU RAISE A BLACK CHILD?

From the dead. With pallbearers who are half as young
as their faces suggest and twice the oxen they should be.
Without a daddy at all, or with a daddy in prison, or at home,
or in a different home. With a mama. With a grandmama
if mama ain't around, maybe even if she is. In a house, or not.
In the hood. In the suburbs if you're smart or not afraid of white
fear or even if you are. Taking risks. Scratching lottery tickets.
Making big bets. On a basketball court. Inside a courtroom.
Poorly in the ever-pathological court of opinion. On faith. Like
a prayer from the belly of a whale. In church on Sunday morning,
on Monday, Tuesday and every other. Before school and after.
In a school you hope doesn't fail. In a school of thought named
for Frederick Douglass. Old school or not at all. With hip-hop or
without. At least with a little Curtis Mayfield, some Motown,
sounds by Sam Cooke. Eating that good down-home cooking.
Putting some wood to their behind. With a switch. With a belt
to keep their pants high. Not high all the time. On all-time highs
at all times until they learn not to feel and think so lowly of
their aims. To be six feet tall and not under. With a little elbow
grease and some duct tape. Sweating bullets. On a short leash.
Away from the big boys on the block. Away from the boys in blue.
Without the frill of innocence. From the dead, again. Like a flag.

POOL PARTY

for Dajerria Becton

I know the average black boy will go to the pool party anyway. No,
he can't swim. He's a joke, dark comedy about transatlantic history,

but he'll be damned if he misses the chance at seeing some skin,
not intending hers any harm in his hormones, of course. He's only

going where the girls are going, just like I did, in my extra-large
T-shirt and brand new navy blue trunks. And all the girls go there

to be seen, if not praised by a pair of hands holding to their hips
in a dim corner of the clubhouse, near a table stocked with chips,

dip and cans of Coke. I was in that place once: bodies bumping
against music notes spat from the DJ's speaker towers, all of our

ordinary laughter strewn from the ceiling in thin ribbons of voice,
balloons bouncing to the beat beneath the dance floor boards, each

refusing to pop off like a reason for us to run. Black kids learn to
dance so well moving around all the dropping bodies; the situation

can change so damn fast. One moment, I'm eying the girl who will
become my girlfriend, admiring the braids on her head, what she

wears during swim season as a way of trying to protect her roots.
And in the next moment, I'm watching her get taken to the ground

before me, those same braids torqued tightly in his hands, his knee
a knife sheathed in the groove between her shoulder blades. I make

the mistake of a step toward her to help. I make the mistake of getting
too close to justice, get the officer's gun drawn in my face. I make the

mistake of watching the video, again and again and again and asking:
how come only our home movies end this way? And yet I've grown

used to it: sleep so easy at night that I can't even be sure I'm alive,
or that all of the chlorine poured into the pool didn't turn me white.

BLACKNESS AS A COMPOUND OF IF STATEMENTS

If you're black, say *black enough*. And if your favorite MC bit a bullet hard like it
was somebody else's rhyme, say *Suge shot me*, twice over. And if you wanted a
pair of Air Jordan 12's when you were young, say *too many boys have mastered the*

fadeaway. And if your grandmother is the best cook in the history of soul, say
can you give me the recipe before you're gone? And if police make you uneasy,
say *sir* after everything you say. And if your parents decided to split, say *I am a*

statistics major. And if you had trouble making white friends stay friends, say
I don't have a middle name. And if you played two-guard like everybody else, say
"either you're slinging crack rock or you got a wicked jump shot." And if you buried

family, a friend who died in the war, never say his name in front of his mother.
And if you knew what war meant, say *Reagan*. And if money couldn't buy you
respect, say *Henry Louis Gates*. And if you were raised a Baptist but idolized

Malcolm X, say *Denzel got snubbed*. And if you copped Sean John from a hustler
that came into your mama's salon, say *velour*. And if you've known someone
strung out like an ellipses of bone, say *my ghosts can't walk through walls*. And

if you prefer thick women, say *JET*. And if you went to the barbershop to learn
how to be a man, say *fade*. And if you ever see Morris Chestnut on-screen, say
Ricky. And if you watch *Boyz 'N the Hood* and you see Ricky come on-screen,

say the name you're thinking of as long as his mother isn't in the room. And if
you've contemplated dying violently someday, say *wedding bells*. And if diabetes
runs through your bloodline like a train of slaves in the wrong direction, say

Sweet 'N Low. And if you cheered for The Rock over Stone Cold Steve Austin, say *you've got to be the corporate champion before you can be your own man.* And if you call matches of your description brother, say *I am his keeper.* And if you

spit on the Stars and Stripes the day Zimmerman got off, say *I'd trade O.J. for him.* And if Spades is the only game you think to play with a deck, say *doing bids may be inevitable.* And if you're black, say *black enough.* And if not, don't say: *listen.*

AT GUNPOINT

Bones quivering and yet the strings
of his ligaments tighten to the point he can

only stand still—   swallow. Push words
down throat in small, silvery bullets of spit:

> *will I make it*
> *home alive?*

His eyes, syncopating like drum cymbals
in their sockets, seeing all the days, all

the years, tattooed with red x's,
stacked high and set aflame:

> a touch of hand
>   reverses him.

From his ashes: florets
staining the air with cinnamon.

Everything back to seed, back
inside the dark shell of nothingness,

the time before time itself. Yes,
a touch of hand might do it—

revert him to possibility,
                    render him a theory,

a wrinkle in the echo of one big bang
waiting for another to occur,

                    a peculiarity of
                              urban physics

either unsolvable or
not worth solving, unless

                    contrast makes for added
                    curiosity. Cameras. Coin.

MELANOPHOBIA: FEAR OF BLACK

How the moon, sometimes, is a scythe of hard enamel,
sign that somebody may be left better-headless in the dark.

How the threat's description is always bigger than
the actuality, panic a hallucinogen ringing its own alarm.

How a teenage boy becomes a bull, a tough cut of muscle
to cut down, *too much to handle*—a man thinks, tickling

a trigger, pathogens atmospheric among the airwaves.
The deepest violet has bloomed: the police are on high alert.

Home security systems have loudened with consumer
demand. Parents in suburbia are turning down the music,

locking up their liquor cabinets and wine cellars, placing
tracking devices inside their daughters' cars. The city wheezes

a swaying of water-stained glass against the sky, always on
verge of shatter. Telecommuting is the only way of traveling

to good work. Somewhere, in a factory near the graveyard of
locomotives, gears continue turning undeterred by the friction

of bodies—sacrifices ground to dust while trying to stop them
from telling lies of time and progress. Everything came back

around to where it was before. There's a hunt going on—not for witches, but female kinds of canine; corrections has an abundance

of cells available, and all those state-of-the-art circuit boards still don't put themselves together: it's said there hasn't been an

operating system developed that performs as well as they do under intense heat, flesh be damned. And it is: looks *hellfired*.

D.W.B.

Don't panic.

When it happens, turn the stereo
all the way down. If it's dark,
nighttime, turn on the overhead light.

Don't panic.

Keep your hands on the steering wheel.
Never make any sudden movements.
Hold your breath.

Don't panic.

If he asks to see your license,
give it to him; your wallet should be
in sight, not in your pocket.

Don't panic.

Calmly ask to reach into
your glove compartment for your
registration, insurance card, if requested.

Don't panic.

For any other type of question,
keep a tight lip, nod only, then
inquire if you may leave, politely.

Don't panic.

Speak slowly. Speak softly.
Use your best English at all times.
Suggest a hint of cursive in your tone.

Don't panic.

He needs to think you know somebody
significant: the Lord or a good
lawyer. Cochran's ghost or Holy.

Don't panic.

Make him think he'll have to answer
if you don't drive away as dark
as you came into his steel-blue eyes.

If he panics
in cold blood.

FACING THE MUSIC

for Sandra Bland

> *You just slammed my head into the ground. Do you not even care about that? I can't even hear...*
>
> – LIVE RECORDING

My eyes need not be mint to *face the music*—ask my man
Ray, or rather, ask Stevie, who is still here with us to be heard,
just how far an ear can go. I don't know if you believe in
Sundays, sir, but from where I stand in my croc skin shoes,
my pinstripe suit and matching hat tipped just so, I say sound,
that slight, polite interruption of still air, is the atom of
everything worth loving in this world, and every person.

People assume that God has hands—like our own hands,
which are used to touch each other's lives in cruel or
unusually beautiful ways. But, again, it is only assumption.

Yet we know, in the lakes of our bones and from this book
tucked under my arm, that God has a voice, as a poet does,
and everything orbits said voice like a chorus of charge.
This, I wager, is why we are most excited by what we hear
or at least, can imagine as coming from a kind of mouth.

And I imagine it was one word or another that excited
your arresting officer, something she said, maybe, causing
this commotion outside the jail. Forgive me for my doubts,
sir, but I have seen lies sold as law before, as the lone star
in the blackest sky effectively guiding us into iron shackles.

I have seen a routine traffic stop become a routine for aspiring
actors before, and recently. Please do not assault my intelligence,
which is always denoted by the asking of questions. Do not
assault me with your aggressive language. Do not assault me with
those gorgeous hands, as what the charge against her suggested.

But if you must, if what I'm saying excites you to that extent,
take my eyes and nothing else, because I do not need them mint
to face the music. Allow me my ears, because without them I can
only know God through the fear that He is speaking to me and
I do not know to accept His offer of a better place than this.

SuICIdE, ıT'S a suICIDe

Do you remember, Sam? The old days,   I mean. When people believed
in the biceps of trees. Toes   at eye level, mostly men. But now they
all would kill themselves   to be "famous": Twitter-trending, hashtagged,
Instagrammed and   graphed via Google's analytics like the pulse line seen
on a hospital   monitor. They want a celebrity synonymous to what Billboard

chart   bullets signaled back when conks were still in style, not cornrows: and
still   the quick and easy cliché of one bullet to a soft spot of the body, though
these days   there's a bit more flair, an adamant need to go out with a bang to
the second power,   "showing out" for all the cell phone cameras, dead set on
becoming a world star.   I've not seen but have heard of trains recently, or

train stations, I guess, somewhere   in California; I think maybe in Oakland,
San Francisco—something like that. It   happened *just like that*, they say,
quickly, like the train's coming and leaving   and leaving his brunette
body behind, hands clasped and yet reaching for each   other as if to pray
but not quite touching properly. As far as I'm concerned,   they're all

playing dangerous games. They just don't give a damn about   their lives,
the whole heathen lot. Jesus Christ, I mean, they're even   drunk driving into
buckshot nowadays. They're calling 911 when   there's no emergency to be
found, pulling pranks against tax dollars;   they don't call 911 knowing that a
little girl sleeps on a couch with   a murder weapon in the cushions, guarding

it with her own body in   illegality. I doubt I'll visit Detroit anytime soon,
not even to catch   nine innings at the house Cobb built, and he's my favorite
player!   And I don't think I'll ever get popping "Skittles" or whatever new
name   they may be calling it now, knowing the overdose is coming. I won't ever
get   their trying to grab a gun if they're not completely committed to shooting

themselves   with it: I say spare the poor man all your hard work, you know?
Always passing   the buck. Always taking the buck out of an honest man's
hands. I can't fathom   absurdity such as stealing cigarillos only to empty
the paper to smoke another leaf   that kills like tobacco from Carolina does.
I fail to see why a woman with a death   wish would give her child to anyone

other than honorable officers of the law. There   is no rhyme, no reason to it,
to anything they do, really. I'll say this: if the heart is   a fruit of blood, theirs
are spoiling strangely en masse, becoming something to be   tossed away,
and Sam, you know better than anyone there's no money in   that. Not like
in the old days. Remember? When they did their jobs   without a complaint?

MEDITATION ON THE CASUAL USE OF HANDS

for Eric Garner

7:39 A.M.—I wake in a mood, my bedroom suffused by a soft blue hue, the song of distant sunlight and low-hanging clouds. I leave my girlfriend to rest a few minutes more, her mind filling in the space between prayer and flesh. I throw on my bathrobe and walk downstairs. I look at myself in the mirror through lenses of dust; discard my robe, my sweatpants, my yellowed T-shirt with a hole to the right of my left nipple, eight or nine millimeters across. I gently twist the faucet handle on its neck. The water is faintly warm, like spit, and takes the smell of my beast-body down the drain with it; my hair gets washed—adored with shea, massaged with my palms and a passing thought or two. I dry off, brush my teeth, head upstairs and throw earth tones over earth tone like a funeral. I depart for work after kissing my girlfriend, still filling my outline in the mattress with more valuable light. I catch the PATH train into Manhattan. It's that rare day I have a seat, which is good, because I forgot my orthotics and my feet are tired from weeks of trying to take stands. I sit next to a swollen brother, but we don't talk, choosing to listen to our headphones until we exit the train. I walk the usual seven blocks, stopping on the way to grab a low-fat cream cheese bagel, tiptoeing around suits on the sidewalk smoking cigarettes, a single at a time. After arriving at the office, I boot my laptop and grind through a long day of meetings held over thin wires. I run into college friends when I pick up a burrito for lunch; I smile at them without concern for what showing my teeth can do. After eating, it's back to hustling. During a bathroom break, a white friend living in Atlanta, who is usually just a friend, texts me: *no indictment.* I text back something approximating anger, but my actual demeanor is more like *word.* I chat with a certain few co-workers later in the day. We're all upset and say so in low voices so our colorful language isn't overheard: *word.* When the work is no longer urgent, I go home. I get a seat on the train again, sitting next to a slender brother playing *Grand Theft Auto: San Andreas.* I don't say anything; just watch his polygonal avatar tote machine guns, think to myself: *word.* When I get off the train in Jersey, I can hear my girlfriend's sister's white boyfriend playing violin on the train platform. Usually, I just think of him as my girlfriend's sister's boyfriend, or as himself, but there's a thin wire in me that's been tripped, and not in the name of classical music. When I get above ground again, my phone buzzes to life: a text telling me to make dinner tonight since she's coming home late. I reply with something equating loosely to *word,* and with that same ease, my praying mind fills my gut with chicken. My hands follow its lead, casually, flouring the cold and the raw. This is how I've been taught to stomach death.

MEDITATION ON BLACK DEATH ENDING WITH AN X-RAY

for Freddie Gray, for Baltimore

Elegy: lament for the dearly departed: an act of dedication or tribute: a monument best made with wet tongue and warm blood: when the bow of a name slides over tightened vocal chords: movement as over violins playing a song of remembrance: they were here: alive: until they died: it was the white rock and the whitewash what did it: the whitewash and the projects' lead paint: the projects' lead paint and the lead: the lead and the gun: the gun and the hand: the hand and the foot: the foot and the other foot: the other foot and someone other's: someone other's and then another's: maybe they marched and marched and marched against some young man's spine on some old "marching" orders: in some cases a van is foot enough: its doors mirror a thug mouth: shut tight: not speaking on how he snapped in half:

the video only caught his screams: body limp while being loaded:

everybody is screaming now: taking to the streets: marching on nobody's orders: the human heart is its own beating drum: stethoscopes say there's a thin line between house parties and war: even gangsters boogie to freedom songs: folks are trying to "get free" out here: the free water is flammable but they drink it anyway: they said all they got left is the fire in their bellies to keep warm: they all dark over there: like a fire ate them alive: they are the color of burning: smoke: cloud formations: gone with the wind wherever it takes them: a better place: into the lungs of the Lord: menthol lover: going off X-ray: through a thicker skin: viewing holy organs: what play the notes of life: interplay between light and shadow: a point bullet-pointed: bang bang: black.

MEMORANDUM

for Laquan McDonald

To: ~~Sr. Marketing Manager, McDonald's Corporation~~ ***white folks***
From: ~~Creative Director~~ ***why does it matter?***
Date: November 25, 2015
Subject: ~~McDonald's Holiday Campaign~~, Urban Demo

~~As always, we chose from many other options.~~ Our core concept is "black reality"~~—think of a reality TV~~ segment shot from inside a motor vehicle, capturing the subject in real time and real terms with a grittier lens. ~~You are going for young. Urban. These people are mobile. They move quickly. They want convenience and expedience. They prize value above all: bang for buck,~~ a buck for a bang. That's the play for this particular market. There needs to be some authenticity here ~~as to what is presented and who is represented~~.

Here's the scene, seen through dash cam:

Nuclear, ~~African-American family~~: Mama ~~(early 30s). Daddy (early 30s). Son,~~ Baby Boy ~~(eight years old). Daughter, Baby Girl (five years old).~~

She had Baby Boy young. Teen mom. Got taken away when he was three. State-warded. Foster-homed. Great-grandmothered. Went back. Boyfriend-abused. Taken away again.

~~Daddy drives while~~ Mama applies ~~some make-up using the visor mirror.~~ ***for legal council*** ~~Baby girl~~ rides backseat ***with Baby Boy's body***, making up songs to ~~entertain~~ **keep** herself *from crying*. Baby Boy looks ~~longingly out the window~~ **dead** when *the first bullet hits him in* ~~his stomach growls and breaks Baby Girl's~~ rhythm, *one one-sixteenth note*. Baby Boy catches glimpse of the ~~iconic~~ golden ~~arches~~ *light* in the distance and promptly asks to go ~~to McDonald's~~, sparking the following ~~dialogue~~:

~~Mama~~ *The Mayor's Office*: "do you have McDonald's money?"
~~Baby Boy: "I got four dollars I been saving."~~
~~Daddy: "Well, that's enough for all of us."~~
~~Baby Girl: "bada bop bop baaa"~~

(cut away to still shots ~~of various Dollar Menu items and special promotions~~) *for the evening news: video frames, Van Dyke's mug shot, the Burger King where security footage of the shooting was boosted from.*

~~We look forward to hearing your feedback on the concept!~~ *Stay woke!*

—*Management*

SPELL CHECK QUESTIONS THE VALIDITY OF BLACK LIFE

Amadou [Diallo]: *did you mean dialogue?*
> Surely. Back and forth 41 times those guns went
> between one another, debating red or blue, and
> yet, ineffectual in stopping the calamity, but so
> goes politics.

Ousmane [Zongo]: *did you mean Congo?*
No difference: one is a nation of darkness, the
other an anthem of darkness. Just beat the drum,
damn it. Beat the drum.

Sean Bell: *did you mean Sean Bell?*
> With every pound he put into that marriage
> proposal, a toll he paid for a ring to mean
> something more.

[Tarika] Wilson: *did you mean tarlike?*
Is God white?

Oscar Grant: *did you mean Oscar Grant?*
> Tell me. What good reason could I have for not yet
> visiting San Francisco other than him when I
> already make people shake wherever I go?

[Aiyana] Stanley-Jones: *did you mean Aryan?*
No, because holocaust's face must always be that
of a victim, of a young girl.

[Ramarley] Graham: *did you mean Bob Marley?*
No, because Mr. Graham didn't actually shoot the
sheriff; the deputy was wounded by friendly fire,
don't be fooled.

[Trayvon] Martin: *did you mean traction?*
Yes, in the way that lynching, the first
quintessential American sport, has regained its
footing among a younger generation—no robes
worn, no fouls given, not a whistle to blow.

[Rekia] Boyd: *did you mean riskier?*
Of course. There may be nothing riskier than being
a black woman in America: because of who you
are, because of who you love, because.

[Shantel] Davis: *did you mean shunted?*
Not with how that blood flowed, going wherever it
damn well pleased.

[Sharmel] Edwards: *did you mean shame?*
Yes.

[Kimani] Gray: *did you mean kimono?*
I did indeed, if ignorance is a kind of silk.

[Renisha] McBride: *did you mean relish?*

Only the day we heard the word *guilty* and wept
from the barrels of our brown eyes what felt like
water, where before there had been only dust.

Eric Garner: *did you mean Eric Garner?*
Nobody did, but it happened by someone's hands,
stupid drunk with something, yet never bitten by a
cuff.

Mike Brown: *did you mean Mike Brown?*
No. I meant Hulk Hogan, clearly.

[Tanisha] Anderson: *did you mean tarnish?*
Accurate.

[Tamir] Rice: *did you mean tamer?*
As in, not twelve years old, but eleven? Ten? Nine?
Would that have been tame enough?

[Cort–]: *did you mean cortisone?*
Well, now that does sound mighty glorious, a shot
to the heart I wouldn't mind taking.

PO-PO POSTLUDE

remixing Tupac Shakur and Kendrick Lamar

Ferguson's police and municipal court practices both reflect and exacerbate existing racial bias, including racial stereotypes. Ferguson's own data establish clear racial disparities that adversely impact African Americans.

–UNITED STATES DEPARTMENT OF JUSTICE

Some say the blacker the berry, the sweeter the juice.
I say the whiter the jury, the tighter the noose.
She say the darker the flesh, then the deeper the roots.
He say the bigger they come, then the bigger he shoot.

He say the bigger they come, then the deeper he roots.
She say the darker the flesh, then the tighter the noose.
I say the whiter the jury, the bigger their juice.
Some say the blacker the berry, the sweeter they shoot.

Some say the blacker the berry, the tighter the noose.
I say the whiter the jury, the deeper its roots.
She say the darker the flesh, then the bigger he shoot.
He say the bigger they come, all the sweeter: like juice.

The bigger his juice and the tighter his roots,
much sweeter as he shoots, deeper in: his noose.

GHAZAL ON THE CUSP OF RAGE

Whereas measures of masculinity are so often predicated on size, and
you look the part of a big-stick boy, be warned my brother: walk softly.

Your name can be a smoke ring risen from the homie's lips, a hit of weed
dulling the pain of your absence due to a fatal hit, outlined in chalk softly.

Cameras never saved anyone from the dogs, the clubs, the fire hoses; you
hear your grandmother's wounds whisper slurs in the night that stalk softly.

She says the '60s weren't long ago, now in her late 60s and dark enough to
remember, praying that God orders your steps away from harm, talks softly.

The stakes are high, brother. We all understand that this is your time to take
a Christian's stone to the heart. Be strong but refuse first throw: balk softly.

The choice here is to do what is expected of you, or not. The cop's is the same.
Tomorrow can be tomorrow, or yesterday: face down on the sidewalk, softly.

Tomorrow, telephone and tell us you looked each other in the eye, even if
only for a second, then come home safe and sound, proud: a hawk, softly.

One day, a child will come to you, your uncanny afterimage, wearing a plastic
badge, pretending a police officer. You'll kiss his cheek. Nod yes. Talk softly.

FEELING FUCKED UP

after Etheridge Knight
for Walter Scott

Lord, they done did the damn deed again   took him out
like   *POOF* like ace   *BOOM*   *COON* like   *WAP* like
motherfucker   he might've been kin you know? like   I'm saying
neither of us can   could   run for shit   guess a cop's shot ain't
gotta be worth spit if he gets eight of them   damn   just ate shrimp
now   it's everywhere   it's dark outside my window America
is everywhere look   this brother ain't coming back none of them
coming back turn yours on a coward they'll prove who they really
are   scared of   is you telling me I went four long-ass days
without knowing he died   that I got my tail light fixed the same
damn day he faded out in broad daylight after getting stopped
for a broken tail light? did I drop $275 just to keep living my
got-damned life?! I got work in the a.m.   but what for? who
I'm feeding? Walter Scott have kids or not? they caught them
bastards on tape   planting the Taser   next to a body
handcuffed to its own color   to lifelessness itself   motherfucker
I can't even   I need a woman   to hold me tonight a good
woman like she would bury me with her own hands good if
I bit the bullet kicked the bucket of blood over I   need Jesus
some Kanye *College Dropout*   tonight I   really need
some liquor   for them to stay outta my face with all
their *oh my God!* every day they kill my God just a little bit
more believe that my brother   it took a camera for all
y'all to believe this was possible but why?   still ain't enough

why?   my background check   clean like   *tabula rasa* like you
can be white on black   and free black on anything and
dead   in jail for life   *sick dopeness*   I got it don't worry   fuck it
I got it   cable news is gonna have field days with this one
and the next   man fuck that   if I'm being completely honest

fuck every Facebook "like" on that video fuck every share fuck
every stock that goes up tomorrow fuck the NRA fuck elephants
and donkeys and trees fuck all the primaries and the general
fuck another White House press conference fuck every
bald-headed bird in the sky fuck "democracy" fuck oligarchy
fuck racism fuck sexism fuck heterosexism fuck classism fuck
the police state fuck law and order if that's what it takes
fuck the drug of war fuck the war on drugs fuck good
people going quiet fuck pure evil fuck the part of me that wants to
forget fuck forgetting fuck not forgetting fuck death fuck my life
fuck every single thing in sight till we all make it all   right.

IN CASE I STILL

for Alton Sterling, Philando Castile & Korryn Gaines

I've been here for hours. Maybe days. Maybe
months. Maybe years at this point, sitting in the dark.

My TV's one big eye is Aryan blue, makes my skin glow
bruise purple and ghostly inside its unflinching gaze.

My TV has a loud mouth and won't keep my name out of it.

Today my name is Alton. Today my name is Philando.
Today my name is Korryn, but on air they mispronounce it

Hillary; my name is something used to spook
other spooks like me: dead
tired, bags heavy under my eyes wide open and veined—

red from fatigue from corner to pupil so all I learn to see
is blood. And I didn't even watch the video.

This time.   And I didn't even talk about it.
This time.   And I didn't even post about it.
This time.

                        There was a song spinning in my head,

but it's gone now.   There was a shotgun burning in my hand,

29

but it's gone now.   There was a fatherly yearning in my heart,
but it's gone now.   Bye bye, baby boy,

     girl.   But my body remains a portrait of grief, I guess.

If it's not remains. If they haven't moved it to the morgue, then
the witness stand, then out of your thoughts completely.

Please, if you care as much as you say, call on me in case I still
have sense enough to answer, weight undead enough to move

from my seat and use productively like units of silver. Transact
not against me Samaritan: spare me pictures, let it click when I pray for

clique, when I need understanding, like today, when I needed you
like I need blood and you couldn't even remember my name.

AVIOPHOBIA: FEAR OF FLYING

Aside from chicken, dipped in flour then fried, there is
an absence of wings here. Here: a hunger—dark, deep

south on the map of the soul. Here: the migration of avian
to mouth, how bones framing former lives are picked apart

while tasting a pleasure to whetted teeth, a klan of pearls. This
is the only way fowl flies—brought airborne to be swallowed

by something that towers over it in stature, that stands several
altitudes of power above sympathy, that rivals the wingspan

of a violent belief, how far it can reach, with ease. And people
can be victimized just the same, taken to the shadow of a throat

as easily as whiskey, done so without being dead first, though
death is promised down the hatch, in the hatching of a plan,

as in the case of that colored man they pulled out of the coop—
where poverty lays eggs in the nest of a black woman's pelvis.

The clucking among the prey was that he'd been picked up
for doing away with a woman, pale as sugar, that lived

by his mama's stay. The crowd came, of course, eager
for the feeding. They cut off his undesirable parts—

fingers, toes, a larger dangling. Stabbed him, shot him
until he stopped struggling. Beat the meat tender.

Strung him up bark to be eaten by wide eyes, a heavy
growling in the wind. What they did to him was foul—

guilty or innocent, their lips licked all the same. We
never forgot the space between his feet and the ground.

PRAISE SONG FOR THE BLACK BODY ENDING IN THE THROAT OF A SWALLOW

Praise the black body. Make ode to its many wounds,
those second and third and fourth and fifth mouths
preaching parables about rocks and slings;
note their clever entendres, how even when
tonguing the molasses of death, they
rhyme in a practice of healing and nursery.
Pray for that type of faith, for the will to remain
fruitful in a world past harvesting
and without a moon to speak of that keeps
the secret of what really happened
that night. Be thankful it swung
and swings for all of you on the cusp,
wearing your more friendly tans,
speaking your not-yet-perfected English. Wish
your own scars heal half as well, but don't
lambaste the liquor that cuts through the air
to your nose. Kiss its lips, but also kiss its back,
because it bends under the past
yet doesn't break. Practice the gait,

> what can be described as both
> gangster and gentleperson at once, pretend
> its rhythm with your feet wherever you go but
> cite the source and pay the royalties. Marvel
> at how it throws itself against a sound,
> utterly fearless, how it hears everything coming

before you do. Thank it for that
warning, the one that saved your life
for others to love. Build monuments to that,
its greatest anatomy of all,
with bars of gold. Go to church in it
and find Jesus, talk to him meekly
about the audacity of combs,
but don't pull his locks. Praise
his devotion to the dirt, make ode
to his many wounds, metaphors and
also not. Forgive yourself, because
you didn't know what you'd done, and now
finally understand, acknowledge all of what
is owed: African that American hallelujah,
don't swallow it unless within a swallow's song.

CHARLESTON

for the innocents massacred at Mother Emanuel AME Church

Nine confirmed dead: the blue backlighting
from the computer screen underscores their black faces
and the rows of teeth therein lit like vigil candles.

Tonight, genuflect seems the fool's gambit—
I recite their names one by one in the shape of a circle,
but I don't receive an acknowledgement in thunder
from above; I'm left only with the begging of two palms
pressed together and the proof it wasn't enough.

My body, a stack of mirrors, falls through itself.
I am several nouns over the course of descent:
her silver whistle, her public library card,
his set of starter hair clippers humming
into the darkness with no plugs in a wall.

I crash through the grey of the matter, go
cleanly through the roof of the church without
making a hole tracing a curious sparrow,
but like a holy bird, I land softly on my feet.

All the expected ornaments are here, I see—
the stained-glass windows overlooking the pulpit,
and two paintings of Christ on the adjacent walls,
Crucifixion and *Resurrection*, and all nine
of their bodies on the ground, not quite cold.

I pick up an annotated student Bible, looking
for Jesus's words for Lazarus, but struggle
because all the text inside is red, still fresh.

I move through the heart of the building, noting
the belongings that will house their ghosts.

Here are the church fans for Sunday service
next to her foot. Here is the sentimental wallet,
holding the pictures of two blossoming girls.
Here is a small wooden cross affixed to a ring
of keys that could open any of many doors.

Here, their scuffed glasses. His navy backpack,
his Chicago Bulls snapback, his black and red Sony
headphones, familiar-looking, looping lyric—Nina,
voice strained through wire, singing *blood on the leaves*
blood on the leaves, blood on the leaves, the bright
face of his smartphone jukebox glowing unattended:

> *Missed Call: Tyrone.*
> *Missed Call: Torrence.*
> *Missed Call: Dominique.*
> *Missed Call: T.J.*

I pick up all their many things
and lay them in a line at the altar.

I find cloth that had been reserved for clergy
and choir in a closet close by, draw them over
the six women and then the three men. I weep,
and I weep, and I weep. And I ask the rhetorical
question *why?*, but this time, receive an answer:

> *I'm here to kill*
> *black people*, he says—

standing behind me. I sweat a bead of blue light.
The thunder enters the back of my head and exits
my mouth in the manner of prayer. I disperse
like a cloud split by lightning, charged electrically
by race: I'm erased. Surely. Completely. Gone.

Like I wasn't even there.
Like I wasn't
even
there.

STATE OF THE UNION

I see it in the American who served his time... the protester
determined to prove that justice matters...
—BARACK OBAMA

As it stands now—right now—I want
                              a divorce   from everything.

This isn't some "mommy and daddy don't love
each other anymore" angst; I was, in fact, born this dark.

I know this body isn't safe anywhere it goes,
                              under any circumstance.

If an All-American heart attack doesn't take me,
it will be a former All-American who took one too many hits

on the field, who says his prayers and eats his vitamins,
who loves his Second Amendment right first,

before all else, exercises it while exorcising a demon,
as he sees it, shooting rounds square in its heart.

Always an "it." Always "not quite human"
                              when you look into my eyes

with a flashlight and find I've been gone for over three seconds
already. Three minutes already. Three hours already, lying

in the exact same spot on the street. How very sad. How very
sick. How very cyclical, this spinning out of control—

backlash from the far wings, a billionaire with a big mouth,
a time bomb waiting to blow in the shadows, somewhere.

And let me say this: you know nothing of gloom
until you're mourning strangers with regularity,

going to their televised funerals, watching the first
President of the United States of your kind of citizen sing

a spiritual penned by slave-trading hands, the whole scene
a sum up: our American sins can never be paid for in full.

I would never trade my black face for Barack's black face,
even if Michelle came as part of the deal. I'd suffocate

between the walls of power because power wants me dead
or moving decimals further to the right, evangelizing the dollar;

in my most agonizing moments, when the tumor of grief
has engorged, I joke that it's his other half that spares him our fate—

the Kansas girl with the ruby slippers—but I know it's actually
the Secret Service, or maybe even the closely guarded secret

that ever since he told America on live television that a buried
black boy looked like the son he never had, all those growing

years ago, the president has been dead inside. And to that,
I can only say: God bless, God bless, God bless, Barry.

For I know what those hands have signed off on, what
those lips have let slide unsaid into unrecorded history:

all audio-visual broadcasted between both terms lacking
those last kernels of truth that would finally break the scale,

rather than trying to balance it back toward a false calm
some folks lived with but others never could. And didn't.

TELEPATHOLOGY
[tel-uh-puh-thol-uh-jee]

noun, plural – telepathologies

---

1. A subliminally transmitted belief espousing the sub-humanity of certain groups
   of people and deviating from healthy emotional and social cognition.

    b. *Sociology*: Devaluation of human lives through rampant, structurally
       determined acts of violence on the basis of a population's cultural or
       phenotypic traits.

KIDS THESE DAYS

And on the way home from our anniversary dinner,
the gas light comes on, so I pull off Ponce de Leon

and park my automobile adjacent pump. Turn off the
ignition. Hear the rap music fade into the mouth of a

gunshot. I get out of the car; she stays inside, texting.
Darkness has infilled the sky completely. It's Saturday

night, the eleventh hour and change, and I look like a
brother that's got a little money to my name, so I'm

more alert than usual: trip off the wind blowing. And
then I hear the convenience store doors crash against

the wall-brick, the glass rattling inside the frames but
still in one piece. My teeth rattling inside the frame of

my gums but my expression still in one piece of thug–
gish. A wolf pack of young brothers, ranging from eight

to twelve in their faces like a classroom clock in morning
hours, running from the thin store clerk, barking the word

bitch at the man behind them, their shoplifting attempt
prevented, or so I convict, shaking my head just like a

gavel vibrating with judgment: *if their behavior escalates
over time, they might pump this Shell station with shells.*

MEDITATION ON WINGS AND MEETING GABRIEL IN A PHILADELPHIA PRISON

Lot of niggas go to prison
How many come out Malcolm X?
    —DICE RAW

Gabriel? Well, first and foremost, he was a black boy, like me, like
a disproportion of the boys in the room with us, some brutal ratio.

You know, I still remember that first poetry workshop he
joined the class; we were shooting with the brothers on the
Rubik's Cube of love, passing it like a blunt in circle over
a rotation of songs, even hands that twisted necks having
trouble subduing it—the halo that sharing ourselves is.

Dean asked from his corner of the city if I *love* my girlfriend,
because the girls he's seen around there aren't the kind
you give the same crown as your mother: *them jawns be...*

From another corner, mention of a newborn daughter,
how she fits in his hand like a stolen watch, though
we don't speak long about time borrowed or taken.

Then there's another shout, an allusion to the heat
of the color pink. Red nodding. Aaron laughing. Gabriel
writing, pushed against his edges like a point of graphite,
heaven's light making a keyhole of him, the gold cross
around his neck reflecting the rays into my heathen,

              its bottomless color.

When I freed my eyes, I looked upon him from a position
of privilege—right place, right time. I noticed his skin was
both darker and smoother than my own, and our eyes were
mud by birth, so neither could decide which of us was guilty
and which was innocent, who was saint and who was sinner.

I spoke to him—in the way God speaks to emptiness—but he
didn't speak back, the visible clump of a fist nestled between
his vocal chords, maybe the very reason why he was even here,
not more than sixteen years old and behind bars like a rapper's
persona. Hopefully the kind who name-drops Malcolm X. All the
verses we mull, maybe, his own Elijah: his new wings, of gauze.

TUPAC SHAKUR'S LAST WORDS

He looked at me and took a breath to get the words out, and
he opened his mouth, and then the words came out: fuck you.

—CHRIS CARROLL, LAS VEGAS POLICE OFFICER

Before the penitentiary, as
he would come to often sing but not quite sing,
she, herself, was the prison: her hair a mat of barbed wire,
African-like, like the sound of her taken name to the jury. And she was
also the bond of words, the mortar   of an unshakeable voice. She was
the first wall, and he left a crack in   her. In the crack, he later found a rock;
in the rock, he found a ghost with   his eyes and a holy word run through
the mud of what she had become. A   few words, actually. There was *love* and
thug and *bitch* and *free* and *sister* and   *mama* and *racist* and *die* and *God* and
enemy and *Hennessy*, which he was   known to share with the neighborhood—
every neighborhood—rocks on their
person, iron under their wrinkled pants.
And he would take those holy words he
found, rearrange them like books of a
Bible, and them boys thought his baritone
fit for preaching, so it became his hustle,
and his flag, and his woman, and all three
will surely do a brother in if he ain't careful.
It'll put his most compassionate lyrics on
trial against her word and his most misogynist,
weigh his final sentence against a dead child,
set him up for a couple chains in New York City,
or really just to put him in his place, start whisper
of him being raped in jail for good measure. Then
he, himself, becomes the prison. Then there is yet
another crack. In the crack, he finds holy words, runs
them under gasoline, sets fire to them. He ties threats
around his mind like a bandana, throws his body like a
rock against any and everything: the policeman walking
up to the car riddled with holes like a flute, the celebrity leaving him with quickness, red
carpeting the shotgun seat, myth making home of his newfound hollow. And he looks to
the officer, his brother's pitiless keeper, with eyes a glint of polished steel. He opens his
mouth, and out of his mouth comes a sparrow. Out of the sparrow comes a bullet. Out of
the bullet, a fragment: *forgive you.* And like that, his mama felt the roots coming free of
her dreadlock, a letting go, as *7 Day Theory*, despite the prayers, was just another album.

BIBLIOPHOBIA: FEAR OF BOOKS

It was written: the alias he's taken to like a real name.
His weight in bare skin and bones. A statement of condition

as one expects to read on eBay auctions—*like new*—
penned next to a price for the body, but not for the head.

The head is an empty grave the rest of him will retreat to
when he reaches the end of his wits and says *no mo' suh*—

but for now, what rests on the ledger's pages is
of indecipherable importance to him. The letters, simply

miniature skeletons of sequenced sounds he's heard in his past,
harbingers of a certain death he does well to duck

by playing dumb or at least compatible to the orders
of his legal holder once the auctioneer has announced sold

and he pretends that he is not shrinking between his legs
or everywhere else. That word is a familiar one, what split him

from the woman he was not allowed to call *wife* within
earshot of a whip. She had been a lighter laborer, a house hand,

even learned to move her own in the figure of her name
as the young mistress of the plantation taught her to

in an illegal act of honey, but when found out, Massa licked
the ink from her fingers after forcing a sign off on her own sale.

He kept the children. Her children: conceived with him or him,
withheld in poor syntax and even poorer spirits; that whole family,

generations later, still un-graduated and having books closed
on them, each ending with them behind bars, bar coded.

THE HOOD

+ + + + +

In the moonlight, a steeple of cloth crowns
the head of a good, church-going man. Pay little mind
to his serpent's tongue. His jagged teeth, deteriorated
from chewing coal. His scornful eyes as bloodshot
as the momentum of a bullet through soft tissue.
Take his word that the rope was tied of good
intentions, tied of great love for country, for family,
for manhood. In imitation of Christ, he carried
that cross here on his back. The fire set to it is not
hatred; Moses will testify it is the healthy fear of God.
Our brother in a gentler nature is only reminding us
of our proper place. And in Sunday affection, we call him

our *Hood*.

+ + + + +

Come dawn, all the colored kids wipe ash from eye.
Pack their schoolbags. Walk past the statuesque making
monument of the corner in front of the liquor store,
past the Pigeon Man passed out on the sidewalk. Trace
the dance of a Christian prayer across the busiest streets.

In their classrooms they read the same books that taught
their grandparents, both things kinds of expository, unhinged
at the spines from life without retirement, just like
the old janitor, sanded down to bone. His hands, callous.

If one could count the splinters that have retired in them
from pushing mops and brooms day after day, they'd have
ample to recreate the accessory of the messiah's end,
what set mold for gold chains of rapper fame.

+ + + + +

While we sleep, he knocks against the window,
shouting epithets, making threats. Fires a few gunshots
into the air for effect. We don't go outside. Don't
confront him brandishing a pistol of our own.
Don't call police, because the police are already
here keeping order. We simply wait for Law

to pass.

+ + + + +

Around here, black men disappear without notice,
never return from the liquor store a mile down the road.

The rumors will spread, say he went for cigarettes,
but in the end, became smoke drowned in wind.

Funeral held in the church a few blocks away
from Big Mama's house, its steeple a historical
allusion in the distance. Everyone passed his casket
dressed in dark, unmistakable ethnicity, even
the men crying as fluently as faucet handles turn,
the rope burns on his throat well hidden by a necktie.

+ + + + +

When night fell again, more shots. A couple
windows broken by the butts of shotguns. Fires
ignited on crosses. We slept through it all,
our bones of rock, the word in his mouth red hot,
hateful, yet warm enough to live with: the fire
a tent is pitched around in brotherhood
wherever we go that also reminds us why

our blood is easy shed.

BLK-on-BLK

White men can't jump   me, or at least, they'd think thrice
before they tried to; I can wear a chain around my neck and still be
off one: that is black magic. Another hallmark trick is disappearance,
completely. Camouflage. Where does my shadow end and my body
begin? On the lip of the moon, my dude—it's his law alone above the
night. Yes, we started substituting "ninja" for "nigga" for this and yet
another good reason:

                        the way we splatter blood like liquid swords
and you see none of it, or choose to ignore it, or shame our codes of
colors and local synonyms. But believe me, we all want to go out the
honorable way. Swinging, to a rugged beat, bumped in the brand new
whip we jacked, named so for the lash the base snaps violently into
our chests, pushing us deeper into the not-yet-broken-in leather. And
if building men paid anything like building cars, we'd do it even more,
I promise you; I say even, because we already do plenty—

                                and you
destroy them all, telepathically, with telecom and what not. Make the
women of us sell themselves for free meals and "horse hair" and skin
lightening creams, and simultaneously, you sell the algorithms of their
curves below market value, and I think: *if only ninjas could hustle that
damn hard and get away with it...*

                        because it's hard to have a beating
heart behind jail cell bars shaped like white sickles. Hard like teeth are
when you sock a jaw with a hand playing the charade of a rock, and not

rock like *crack*, but rock like what welcomes the playing of heavy metal
to end a fight: maybe before it even starts, before the school bell rings,
or after it rings, or the head is just always filled with the ringing of red
and you can't hear not one thing else. This is how it speaks its presence:

the anger beyond the anger, the adhesive between our lips as we stand
before a camera flash. We haven't learned how to smile when we mean
evil. We know deeply this is the difference between us and the inverse
of and the reason our faces become problems of subtraction—the minus
signs of our mouths. Believe it: we can do math. We will do the math
for you, even. Keep even keel. Shoot and shoot and shoot and shoot and
shoot like it doesn't kill us too, by which I mean one bullet one black boy
fires goes in two directions at once. Forwards, backwards: a trap.

MAKING A FIST

after Naomi Shihab Nye

I already knew how to, just as my eyes knew their
color before ever formed as windows to my fears.

   Before showing my heart, a glass vase full of white
   lilies, falling to the floor of my stomach, shattered

into some thousand reflections of cowardice. I swept
the debris aside with bare hands, caught a shard of

      scorn in the palm, in the bowl where I hold feed for
      songbirds. I shut hand tightly to stymie the bleeding

deep inside myself. Lost my better consciousness in red
like a horned-head to the whisper of a matador's cape.

      By the time that I recover, the wine of life already
      trickles from his mouth, the weight of a prophecy

fulfilled tied to the end of my wrist. My entire existence
spent trying to avoid this inevitability, or turn its path

      into my own jaw, but seen so vividly, as if it occurred in
      the dream of a god of war. Black boy must be re-taught

to grind rock into dust, scatter intent to the wind; the stone
I cast could always be a punctuation: lead slug moving heat

      through my cold spaces, no strength remaining to draw
      fingers into the intent of a hammer, the proverbial nail.

YOU'RE ONLY AS HEALTHY AS YOU FEEL

This is how it should be done: place the pistol, loaded,
in the nightstand nearest where the last letter of the alphabet

repeats itself.   In the same drawer, set a stolen hotel Bible:
the New International Version.   In the event of bodies colliding

in a fender bender, stow away some condoms that can survive
the tread of a hunger pang.   It might even be worth it to stash

a notepad and pen there if you're a sensitive type, find yourself always
at the tipping point like a bottle full of tequila.   Don't forget

the pills, either.   Hold those within reach of a gasp for air—
pop them all, watch the lines blur and black swallow every other color like

a ghetto music.   Have a dog around, too.   A big dog with a mouth
the size of a city, teeth jagged as a skyline's tracing.   Two dogs, even.

Two big ones.   Think about Pit bulls, Rottweilers.   Don't bank
large sums of money in the house; it's trite and the back can't cope with

that kind of mattress anyhow.   Before hitting the sack for good,
make sure the house is empty, except for the dogs, of course.   Check

to see if the gun is resting safely in the nightstand drawer.   If not
there, check inside your mouth, by the dogs' water dish, maybe under

the toilet hood. Lock all your doors and windows tight.   Keep light on
in the hallway to scare away any dark figures.   Pour yourself a glass

of ice cold water and bring it bedside.   Read scripture and pray.
Add several milligrams to make it happen faster, maybe not wake up

too sore, back due for a good massage.   Remember to put on a rubber
before the night consumes you, in case a blessing comes in your sleep.

AMERICAN TERRORISM IN SEVEN ACTS

I.
Survival tactic: poor movie etiquette.
I keep my cell phone on silent, never off.

As people file into the theater,
I locate the exit signs. Record them
to heart like a drumbeat.

Sip a cool beverage as walls close in,
the seats on either side of me taken by
the silhouettes from gun ranges.

The speakers blast violently.
I go deaf for a moment or two.
See a demon hatch from the
eggshell of a skull. Pinch myself.

II.
The audience claps. Heads home
without a single prayer uttered.

By the time I'm sitting behind
a steering wheel I have forgotten
the value of life, something measured
when fear is on opposite balance.

Fear: that sensation known when
a cop stops my car while I am dressed
in my skin; what subsides as my
diction graduates, my purple English
substituted for, possibly, a purple bone.

I got off with a ticket and
an attitude. Drove slowly from
there on, my radio lying low
like a fitted cap over the eyes.

Before long, I hear sirens again.
Look in the rearview mirror, see nothing.
I'm the one closing in. Meeting fate.

III.
Gangs, said in an apathy that
could drive men to murder.

How sad. To that boy, it must have
sounded like a bomb exploded,
the limb of a family tree blown off.

That was the story in Boston,
in Oklahoma City, but the reporters
don't mention a terrorist here.

IV.
Indifference is figurative language
fit for interpretation like a poem
taught at Columbine High School.

Three dozen shot on the wrong
side of town this weekend; we take
our morning coffee with cream.

V.
It's becoming all too common we cried
when schoolhouse rocked, turned
a choir of blonde angels within minutes.

VI.
It is all too common, the avoidance
of certain places, certain conversations.

VII.
Disregard of life by any mode is
a concept that wears a suicide vest.

Spade is spade no matter why
it digs the grave it does, so call us
what we are to our enemies.

Stand your ground on that and
kill to protect it. Forget about
walking home from school through
turf wars over grams of rock.

Admit the September move to
New York City never happened
because everyone rides the subway.
The risk, you thought, too great.

WHERE BROOKLYN AT?

Was Williamsburg a conspiracy? Are white folks the real illuminati?

—JOSÉ GUADALUPE OLIVAREZ

I felt safe immediately: got off the L Train,
didn't even smell urine panhandling through
the tunnels like in so many other   arteries
of this insomniac city. I thought this was Brooklyn.
                         I didn't know better.
Walked up the stairs to Bedford Ave, looking
for the restaurant I told my high school homeboy

J. Bedford to meet me at,   feeling safe all the while
for the wrong reasons. I pulled out my phone and
plugged my position into Google Maps,   the cursor
pulsing on screen like   the speakers of a boombox
         holding a window open to stave summer heat,
a scene I lifted from a Spike Lee joint seen years ago.

             The map says I'm in Brooklyn,
that my chicken and waffle spot is less than a mile away
heading north.   I text the homie to see where
he be, but don't get a response; I figure that he's riding
underground, like so many rappers

             cyphering for change in two meanings.
I count the number of folks who walk by dressed in
a code I can understand: snapbacks, low-tops
         or retro Air Jordan's   color-matched

61

to T or cap or denim.   I estimate five
in 50 minutes of waiting, but see a whole lot

     of skateboarders with horn-rimmed glasses and
     women with cigarettes tattooed to their lips.
Bars and few bodegas. Safety.   When J. Bedford
finally arrives, I ask him why the trip was so
long if he lives in Brooklyn.   He says he cabbed,

     didn't even take the train; it would've been out
of the way,   and that spoke about as loudly as the fact
there were no black folks   frying our chicken.
Only eating, paying,   then erasing themselves.

EXHIBITIONISM WITH A DROP OF BLOOD

after viewing Kara Walker's "A Subtlety, or the Marvelous Sugar Baby"

Domino Sugar Factory, Brooklyn, NY

A vulva made of sugar—
his tongue visible with intent to lick,
and I suppose I shouldn't be surprised
that it's possible for a white man
to rape a ghost and get away with it,
not even fathom the crime. I mean,
she was posed like any other sphinx
ready to receive, Jemima as video vixen,
a sweet poison. And we stand there,
quartet of voodoo dolls—being pricked—
observing the observers who pinch their
chins in practiced interpretation, make
juggling motions underneath her breasts,
pose for camera phones. All the while,
her children remain scattered about
the factory grounds, red as wounds,
their faces granulating into historical
obscurity as their mother is made
a third-string noun in their presence:
naked because she was never given
any clothes to work in. And it's clear
I have walked willingly into the mouth
of some type of fox, feel walls of teeth
closing in, ready to crush the bones
of all these slaves into a question
without answer, me along with them,
and the artist, a deist's kind of god.

WHITE, AS TOLD BY BLACK

White: when asked for the umpteenth time why
my hairs curl into bolls, I will tell the half-curious
it is because of the cotton in my blood, waiting
to see if they recognize the fist they just spoke.

More likely, they will demonstrate an illiteracy of
scarred-back stories, smile at me, the menace of their
clean, bright teeth begging complete calm of me akin
to that of my granny handing me her diploma from
Louisville Negro High School, for me, a separate
but equal discomfort: *black*. Again, its opposite:

> a pack of bloodhounds, shotguns, shovels and
> sheriff's badge in star formation. Decades later,
> I'm digging up all the bodies with a thesaurus.

> > I spent my early years with very little contact or
> > context: my schoolteachers, the only examples of
> > the antonym of me. From Pre-K to kindergarten,
> > first grade to second, they, and sometimes God,
> > the only such folk I found outside of ghost stories.

> > Stories from my grandparents, whistling like cold
> > wind in the night, that pulled my consciousness
> > from the river of my blood like a mangled body
> > screaming *Tallahatchie* into the ear of eternity.

> I am an open casket. Read me right between
> the eyes. This right here is wisdom most children
> can't comprehend straight away: the very idea
> of friction. How chalk writes on a blackboard.

At my new suburban school, during art classes,
I drew myself with only one crayon as if I didn't
wear any clothes, the choice inescapable and
Basquiat already ten years gone from overdose.

In Phys. Ed, I jogged, never sprinted. Dribbled
with both hands on the ball on purpose. When
line dancing, I didn't color outside of them and
draw more attention to myself. The black kid is
entertainer by default, just a spec in a white hot
spotlight, and Dave Chappelle hadn't yet walked
away from millions for an imaginary crack pipe.

It took until high school for people to out me
as acutely intelligent, like a scalpel: to learn
I could explain how a word has its black side
without spitting watermelon seeds in their faces.

Before I knew it, they were referring to me
only by my slave name, washing me white,
trying to put a whip in my hand to use against
the other blacks I'm not like, all the while
Obama planning his presidential campaign.

Some time later, I discovered my granddaddy
kept a secret gun in his shoe closet for over
sixty years, an old habit from Mississippi,
and to me, it made complete sense: *white.*

ARTFULLY DODGING THE SUBLIMINAL AND OBVIOUS

What they said was: *you'll get in for sure.*
What they meant was: *affirmative action* is a bitch.

    And what I said was: *maybe, we'll see.*
    But what I meant was: *affirmative action is a bitch.*

Then what I said was: *my test scores top*
the curve, I'm at the top of our class,
so I guess my shot's as good as any.

But what I meant was: *my smarts trump my street*
every time, homie. And what *street* meant was *black,*
even though our streets were the same streets.
    What *homie* meant was nothing.

Then the acceptance letter came. And they said:
congrats! But they meant: *lucky you're black.*

And what I thought, but didn't say was: *lucky there*
was never a whip in my folks' hands. My grandpa
could pass for an ass-whoopin' in Mississippi.

    But what I said was: *thank you. I'm excited.*
    Let's see if the Ivy League really is paradise.

And when I got there, my tour guide said: *welcome!*
And I said: *glad to be here. I'm truly blessed.*

Then they showed me around, told me: *we got
fantastic dorms for freshman to choose from.*

When they got to the one named for W.E.B.
DuBois, they said: *historically African American.*

What that meant was: *most of you
incoming students don't want to live here.*

And I thought to myself: *looks like the projects
of privilege, if heaven had a ghetto.* I said to myself:
I think I'll try to get into one of the high-rise dorms.

But then I was visiting that damn dorm every day,
because I had people there. And I thought: *must be
that suburban conditioning, of being from "there"
and not from "there,"* but then I realized only black
folk go back to the gutters they crawl out of.

Because one of my roommates was white, but
trailer park, and I know rich kids on these grounds
toss out words like *white trash* for his off-brand
and you don't go back to that if you can escape it,

but *white trash* suggests *exception to the rule.*
Because what poor really means is *black or brown,*
though they don't say that in any of my classes.

What they say instead: *correlation*.
What they mean: *causation, as designed.*

> And what I think about but don't speak is how
> me and my homies couldn't get into a party
> because the token had already been played.

And what *token* means is *black but not,*
like erasure of culture, like *he listens to alt-rock*
and only dates white girls, like he won't get
mad if I say nigga when Lil' Wayne is on
speaker because he knows I'm not racist,

so they think. But I say: *forget this party. The music*
sounds wack and Lord knows them girls can't dance.

And what I do instead is go to Crown Fried
over on 40th and Market Street. Grab me
some dark pieces. Mac and cheese. A biscuit.

Campus police are barely over there
this time of night, I think, quietly.

The ghetto expands at this hour, which means
you have to be black to even want to step over there,
black meaning what makes West Philadelphia
a questionable place to attend college, or live in,
or come from with pride and a humbled lip.

THE MELANIN

I walk into a room full of ghosts, their translucent intentions packed
from wall to wall.   I avoid speaking.   There's a human piñata—
a mob victim—hanging in the back of my mouth I don't want them
to see or smell.   Every night I dream about him and every night

he has a different name, one with an urban suffix or an apostrophe.
        Death has a color that's often described as *slimming*; I'm
not actually as thin as I appear.   The wind can't blow me away
and call it *change*. It tries to beat me down over decades like a rock.

A paper airplane rides it through the air, lands in my kinked
hair and catches, to their amazement.   As we study electrical
charges, my head becomes the choice conductor and sometimes
the voltage is more than they bargained for.   They haven't

learned how much water I'm made of, how many slave ships
I've swallowed down the hatch.   My brain buoys the memory
of them above the blood.   At times, they whisper about revenge
but I keep my teeth confined.   I act fitting for a petting zoo,

though it is only because I'm still young.   The parents worry that,
eventually, their girls will see my *gun* and that I'll secure a second.
        Their eyes hawk me closely, so I play a pocketknife: mind my
manners and retract the threat.   I try not to spook the ghosts.

MILEY CYRUS PRESIDES OVER
THE FUNERAL FOR THE TWERK

I'm glad you know that twerking is so yesterday … the new dance
is called "The Nae Nae"… I don't really know the origin. Just my
dancers, the LA Bakers, they taught it to me… so then I started
doing it, which is kinda what happened with the twerking, too.
—MILEY CYRUS

As we gather here today, we do so with heavy bass,
tatted up, J's on our feet, carrying wrecking balls
to tear this church down once we leave—
because sadness in the passing of life
is for boring old white people: wack. This is
a party. This is what The Twerk would've wanted,
I know. I knew her so well. I remember hearing
an old saying, I think from 2-pack, maybe
Snoop D-O-Double-G, that *you live by the gun,*
you die by the gun. I'm not sure how it fits
the occasion quite yet, but let's just say
The Twerk wasn't a gangster or a gangster's
trick—she didn't deserve to go so soon,
but life is hard in the ghetto, I hear
from all my friends in the streets and
struggle. Folks were mad when we started
cliquing like some triggers, were so appalled
by the moving and the shaking, the rump
to bump, but you can't hate on that. If
you got ass, then use it. The Twerk taught me

well. How do you think Robin Thicke became
THAT famous a dick? It was these hips, this
tongue. That was us—me, and her, too. She
was backstage with the Bakers, counting
all the paper pouring in, posting the good word
on Twitter. And all you tweeted back at her
was venom. That girl had a family, she had kids
to feed—Nae Nae, lil' Shmoney—kids who
survive her. And I promise to treat them like
they're my kids, since I loved their mother
so much. I will make sure they become the stars
they deserve to be, so that when they die, they
too can be buried in ivory caskets scrubbed clean
by a toothbrush. Mike Will, make it so. Mike Will,
if you're here, make it so! We can't stop now.

I'M NOT A RACIST

I'm a realist: if I see a pack of hoods approaching, loitering,
acting a littering of public sidewalks, I simply

move to the other

side of the street, play it safe. I keep it on me at all times,
for safety purposes.

In the event of open fire,

you'd be a hazard I told them when I, regrettably, couldn't
allow the lot of them into the party.

We're part of the same

political party, according to all the numbers I've seen.
When I shut the schools down, I was just

doing what must be done

to balance a city budget out of wack. When I put what
I found in his trunk on balance,

it was enough to tip the scale

towards a felony. I used to be a waiter, and they never
tipped very well in my experience.

While we were placing bets,

I noticed him tip his hand ever so slightly and there was
a ~~race~~ face card in it. He didn't seem

like much of a bluffer, so I stood

my ground. *On the grounds of merit*—that's how I got
into Yale. I'm just not that into black

girls, *personally*. I mean, personally,

I don't *SEE* color. I'm so sorry, I really didn't see you there.
There they go, using that word again:

if they can say it, then why can't I?

I can't understand why everybody is so sensitive these days.
I admit, what I said sounded a little bit

insensitive, but believe me, I'm not

a racist. I'm a realist: if I see a pack of hoods approaching, loitering,
acting a littering of public sidewalks,

I simply move to the other side.

I keep it on me at all times, for purposes: *in the event of a
hazard, open fire* I told them, regrettably,

looking at the body splayed before me.

73

HOW DID THEY JUSTIFY THE SHOOTING?

Fired first and fatally. Radioed in that every body within
vicinity with two arms was an armed and dangerous
suspect. Described the face of the suspect according
to their own imagination. Changed the suspect's
description from *woman* to *man* to *black man* to
Superman to *black male* to *blackmail* to *black*,
black, black. Exaggerated the sharpness of his-
her teeth. Fetishized the size of his-her gun.
Invented a gun out of thin air. Gave quote to
their superior officer that the air was thinning.
Couldn't breathe. Panic, attacked. Feared for
their life. Weighed their own life on a scale
against air, against his-her nothing. Said their
weapon was reached for, attention-drew his-her
eyes, had to draw their weapon in cold ink. With
necessary force. With foresight. By sight into the
demon's soul. Because the devil lived within him-
her. Because the devil is a liar. By telling a large
enough lie that everybody could buy it. Bought
their own lie. Stuffed his-her limp body with
dollar bills and let all the good law-abiding
people beat it like a piñata. Laughing all the
way to the bank. Licking the sugar of the law.

TELEPATHOLOGIES

Tell me: how does the mind host its sickness?
Is it hosted anything like how a website is,
the Internet just a cancer spread of ones
and zeroes? Is it like how a mixtape is hosted
by a DJ with a bunch of zeroes behind a one
behind their name? I downloaded a sick
tape off DatPiff not even two days ago,
but what was sick about it? Is it the way
a baritone-mention of *pussy* makes the
mouth wet, or is that just how a word is
born, normalized by biology? Is biology
the reason *Ebony* pops up before all
other exotics in a survey of masturbators,
or is that the symptom of a sickness?
Would you consider WorldStarHipHop
a sickness, or all the site traffic from white
boys watching in the suburbs, as if vitiligo
has gone viral? If I told you a black woman
had her tubes tied tight by television signals,
would you label that sickness idiocy or
call it rational? Does the answer change
if she was scared of having a son end up
like his father, or is the sickness in your
assuming what that means? If I *feel her*
in idiom, does that diagnose me suicidal,
or just afraid of homicide? Is sickness

imagining your death or imagining it
by your own hands? How is that sickness
hosted? Is it anything like how a website
is, the Internet just a cancer spread of
ones and zeroes? Is it infinite in reach,
or is my body the bounds? Am I the host,
a lasting cure only discovered once I'm
disposed of *for good*? When the next of me
makes the nightly news, gone for good
via gunshot, will you be bedridden with
a sickness, or will you step outside, healthy?
Will you develop a healthy fear of your own
shadow? Would that be just? Justice? How is
that agent hosted? Anti-body? Like a cancer?

GHAZAL FOR THE BATHING APE

And any beast that walks on its fists can't be called a man;
   force animal to wade in water, hold bathing of its hands.

Give it body in reciprocal to see if it makes man, maybe
   love: holds it whole, believes it to be a saving of its hands.

If beginning to feel its hands holy, catch ape making ways
   by waves of crime, then pass laws scathing of its hands.

The animal is muscle-bound to drum. When fits of dance
   come, proper grammar won't be a persuading of its hands.

Build a cage for all its boom, bang, bap and onomatopoeia.
   Clasp halos round its wrists or require evading of its hands.

Brute of concealed fangs, urgent threat, jungle manners;
   let it slang its weight till it disappears: erasing of its hands.

Remember, the beast walking on its fists isn't truly a man.
   If it turns unruly, use this here bullet, a staving of its hands.

SIX SHOTS ON FERGUSON, MISSOURI

for Mike Brown

[bang]
      Oil does, in fact, have a color.
Burns easily if provoked by open fire.
      Animates itself a body,
becomes sticky with the humidity of breath,
         can enunciate the words
don't shoot, I am a man.

[bang]
He's lying dead in the middle of the street—dead,
blocking traffic,
a crimson signature incomprehensible on the asphalt.
Who'd they get, there?
The whole block taking a rounder shape about the scene,
the whole block as dark as an avian's kind of murder,
or just murder,
their camera phones shooting in irony,
not quite fast enough for WorldStarHipHop to become CNN,
but enough to make sure the police get proper sketch.
They killed that man for no reason.
Mike Brown is too common a name to disappear,
not that easily. No. They'll tie his bloody T-shirt
to a loose stick and call it a flag.

[bang]
    Sirens sing loudest after sundown.
Ferguson ain't special, man.
        Look—they got young Odysseus.
Loaded his body into an unmarked SUV,
        draped it in a white sheet for good insult.
Nothing has changed, man.
        Missouri was the slave state that compromised
a harmonious union, or did y'all forget?

                                        [bang]
                    A bomb sounds like a thousand people
                    screaming the same thing at once.
                            It's an honest mistake.
                    No justice, no peace? Fuck the police?
                    It's an honest mistake when you're not used to
                                        hearing explosions.
                Only the most seasoned reporters get sent into Gaza,
                                        or Iraq,
                        or anywhere full of oil and open fire.

[bang]
    The QuikTrip, some local stores: puffed out.
Block boys got bandanas covering their mouths,

patterned tongues,
same geometries of defiant language on them.
There's tanks on the street, word is.
Military weapons.
Enough tear gas to make several grieving mothers.
This is beyond protest; it's singeing a noose.
Bet folks can smell the oil burning from DC.
Somebody taps on my shoulder in the airport
as we watch it all on TV: *who died young man?*
I turn to them, my facial sprites of wild
and colorful confusion.
Dr. King was just assassinated.
Can't you tell by the pictures?

[bang]
Never go to the Internet in a moment
of moral crisis.
After a surveillance video from a strong-arm robbery
alleges human instead of angel,
a commenter who refuses his real name will suggest
$50 in cigars is fair trade for six bullets and a funeral.
Funny. Back in slavery days,
an ox like the brother in the video could've fetched more
than five measly tens, but
I don't know why I'd expect a fool to try and grasp
the mathematics of oppression if they've never
seen numbers in the red.

TELEPATHOLOGY
[tel-uh-puh-thol-uh-jee]

noun, plural – telepathologies

---

2. The rigorous study of any and all manifestations of the physical, emotional or spiritual decay derived from internalization of implied falsehoods about the sub-humanity of one's own body or community.

MAMA SPEAKS ON PROFILING

Some folk will always
look at you sideways, their eyes
a slant of sour
opinion, but freedom is
a forward march, baby boy.

Give cheek without cheek;
steadfast sight on glory. Christ
saved you already.
No book thrown at you can weigh
more than all that precious blood.

HOW DID YOUR MOTHER DIE?

She was a ghost from the day she was born.
Arm & Hammer baking soda. Just a hammer
and a strong arm. Head wasn't as hard as his.
The love of him that was hardheaded. Ran
out of milk in her bones. Smoked like the
barrel of a gun. A stray in the summer.
Burying my big brother. Lived outside the
circumference of a horoscope. Ovarian
cancer. Took a breast away and then the
rest after she missed a payment. One
surgery too many. Too many hungry kids.
Eaten. Fish-hooked and tossed back with
no Band-Aid. Drowned. Two handles of
vodka and a steering wheel. In the county
jail. Did her time and got set free for good
behavior. Let go. Impossibility. So dark
that they couldn't even see her. Made a
promise to be at the game. We traced her
body in crayon on a big sheet of paper. Too
much sugar in the bowl of her hips. Chicken
bone. Trying to help. Police didn't search
very long. She didn't want to be found. God
took her. Saying a prayer for me. Explaining
what "forgiveness" means. The sun came up,
and she was an owl's song. *Slow. Like fog.*

after Jeanann Verlee
after Clarie Kageyama-Ramakrishnan

MEDITATION ON SUNDAY TRADITIONS AFTER THE VIDEO LEAKS

for Janay Rice

On Sundays like this: the fearing of God. Football and the oblong
shape of a family. I listen to an old story—about Granny's hair
getting caught in the knuckled-grip of a flame, about Granddaddy's
hands patting flame out over screams of *Alvin*, though his first name
is George and it took me years to figure that out. Unkindness—that
is a flock of ravens in the sky somewhere. Today, I imagine there is
a pot of rice on the stove for my more fickle sister. Mac and cheese
in the oven for me and everybody, fried chicken in a paper bucket
paid for by collection plate: soul food as shadow of the Deep South,
stretching throughout the house, a mix of warm-sweet flour and
musty greens, a scar reflected on fondly, but still a scar. On the TV,
there's the purple of a polished helmet, a bruise of light shined on
our faces, kissing the darkness of our skin. And another darkness is
the truck in the garage that he can no longer drive, what she never
learned to in these many years rooted—but I'm distracted from it
by the absence of my favorite side dish, my first grandchild privilege.
Watching the game, there's side commentary about my granddaddy
playing with the pigskin in his younger days. I can smell a helping of
smothered pork on the counter. As a dry house, there is no alcohol
here, no beer. But there's a recent medical condition, continuing to
erase who he's been except for the mercy of a smile. Windows open
to a breeze, an air of defeat in Baltimore, blowing west to where we
be. I notice the darkness of our skins again, because we can't escape
them, as well as the scarcity of men in this house full of women. In the
spaces between us, there's a question that needs to be asked of every
man by every man, but isn't; my sister nonchalantly recalls our brother

breaking the lock on a door in a fit of manhood once. As she does, I can feel my muscles work, rounding hand to wrecking ball—muscles I had forgotten were there. And here the Baltimore Ravens are on TV after another pitiful Bears defeat, the home-white ghost of Ray Rice in the middle of my eye. There's the moving image of a woman being carried like a lifeless pigskin, of his hand with no fear of God at that particular time, I guess, because the film wasn't taken on a Sunday—because on Sundays there's football to play, the oblong shape of a family huddled around a television set: a circle, but also not—a halo only if squinting.

GYNOPHOBIA: FEAR OF WOMEN

Whether sparing her the rod. Whether sparing neither set of kids
or all: dimorphism, a difference in muscle and its willing use.

The raw-pink question is how a body learns to speak this way,
like a boy, in only blues and purples, with hammers of bone

and skin. In elementary school: mirrors on the tips of shoes,
skirts folding in the wind as the fabric of a pale flag would, and

no one asks how we ever learned to play that kind of horn at such
an early age, before we could even read a hormone's sheet music

in the blemishes of a face. How we could say to her, *you are
so pretty.* Say to her, *do you wanna arm wrestle?* Say to her,

*ain't no girl ever beating me in a game of one-on-one, so
you might as well just be my girl. Honey. Boo. Baby. Doll.*

Such sweet contrivances allow poisons easier swallow—worn
knuckles, any substance that knots the blood or makes the mind

disappear. They say *all is fair in love and war,* no more clever
form of confession there are casualties we expect and tolerate,

casuals: a cupping of ass in the darkness of the nightclub. An
analogy, carnivorous and carnal, hissing *bitch* as she walks by.

How a man stands at altar-head before God and God's mama
and declares that he's marrying his *best friend*—meaning it,

but not how it is prayed, his mouth: a drawer full of knives.
Honeymoon moon: an ill yellow. His hand on the doorknob of

her knee—if she locks her legs closed there will be no more
of him. Hostility can be his sudden turn, or hardly a turn at all.

KEEPING JELL-O

The Bill Cosby thing is so ... awful... It was a badly kept secret in the comedian world, and a lot of us would talk about it.
—PATTON OSWALT

Being a highly processed food, it is built to last. If speaking to the pre-packaged gelatin that comes in plastic cups for individual serving, the product can last in a cold refrigerator anywhere from 12 to 18 months, should it remain factory sealed, and not many secrets can survive that long and still come out so shocking to the taste buds or whatever else. Opening them after the expiration date has passed does not inherently mean the product cannot be consumed, or provide some type of relief, but it may leave a poor taste in your mouth or elsewhere. If worried about taste, consider purchasing the powder mix and then stowing it away in a cool, dark pantry where it can sit indefinitely. When you finally open the package, do not be surprised if it looks like cremated remains. Do not be alarmed if, after consuming, your tongue feels possessed, moves to recite names of women you've never heard of: this has been well documented; it is a common reaction to have.

A BOOGIE NIGHT, AGE 12

The signal from the wireless router cuts in and out like a conscience,
and the image quality on the video is average at best—their bodies,

the two of them, constellations of tiny, tiny boxes, glowing a tad bit
orange, red, what at times suggests harsh touch, excessive pressure

put on skin by skin. Every parental obscenity you believe should be
present is, and in proper number, the geometries bordering on absurd;

their acrobatics, the physics of lust bate boyish breath into buffering.
You jump excitedly around the video to catch the action from all its

different angles, a very certain piece of you protracted in eager study.
Your mouth floods. Your ears sharpen to the point of picking up pin-

drops, like a cat's, just in case the floorboards trace the sound of a
foot. At the end of the clip—is the finish: he stands over her, his hairy

legs split in a victorious straddle and face somewhere out of frame
along with the boom mic. She, on the other hand, kneels on the hard

floor, staring directly into the camera lens—smiles, then licks her lips
and teeth clean: *enthralling*. But even more so? The light in her eyes

was *quiet*,

like it was

waiting to burn.

GHAZAL OF THE CODE

There are rules to this shit, homeboy: being a grown man, making it
happen with these girls out here. You can't step soft like some homo,

with your feelings all twisted and folded like some Pre-K-ass origami.
Girls like edges, man—so stay sharp. Be bold. This sounds dumb homo,

but you're not a bad looking dude at all. Don't take it the wrong way,
I mean. Just saying looks ain't the issue. You just get too glum. Homo-

ish, hurt too damn easily in the heart. Man up, G! Keep your head up.
Walk with swagger. You're packing **HEAVY**. Rule of thumb, homo-

ass comment be damned. Go up to her. Not in a rush. Not in a hurry.
Say something that can be taken as sweet, but not say, ummm, homo

or corny. It's all about balance. Act like they're special and like they
don't matter at the same time, and then bang 'em like a drum. Homo?

No? Aight, then. Just don't act so damn scared! Don't get shook. All
you're trying to do is get some play and keep it moving. *Scum, homo,*

trifling-ass Negro she might call you, but that's on her, fo' real. If it's
any good, a good man keeps it going, I mean, if they ain't some homo.

THE BARBERSHOP

is hallowed ground in hoods across the nation and how could it
not be? I mean, there are so few places, so few situations where a
brother has a blade pressed to his neck, preciously near an artery, yet
knows mercy: its razor-thin pressure point lifting away without drawing

one drop of blood. I mean, even the clippers, well oiled and labor-warm,
hum like an old deacon's lip during devotion if you listen real close.
I mean, the barber steadies my worldly-worry-heavy head with

his hands and you can't tell me that's not how love cuts in close
quarters. I mean, *they* say black folks don't tip, but that's for service;
we tip well for *love*, just ask any one of the fellas that crops our hair as
hi-top, bald fade or other. I mean, when I tell him hit me with a "one" that's

all that needs to be said; said differently, the barber knows every one of my
secrets by the shape. I mean, young and old school players alike all shoot
shit on skirts, straight scheming on sex and other Saturday night jaunts.

I mean, everybody is *straight* while they're up in the shop. I mean,
everybody be eyeing hard whenever she walks through those doors in
sunglasses and a tight pair of jeans, high-cut shorts. I mean, she's cool to
come into the shop, get a cut like everybody else. I mean, I think everybody

there wants to cut her, fo' real. I mean, I know women who can really cut
a brother's hair, hook him up real good, too. I mean, plenty of women
have brothers, have baby boys they bring in to tame the beast of

their kink. I mean, when baby boy finishes getting his hair cut, he's
going to look like her *little man*. I mean, lil' man gonna learn how to
be one in here—when to raise his eyebrows, who for, how to inflect his
fresh line to advantage. I mean, this is the space we pray all our black baby

boys are able to have. I mean, they need to know in what ways Jordan is
God and Kobe, his first disciple. I mean, if they can't play ball, then
thank God they got somewhere else to go and get their hustle on.

I mean, don't it sound like a church when you think on it—full
of sinners but something pure and sacred at the same damn time?
I mean, haven't we made movies about this? Wasn't Ice Cube in it?
Cedric the Entertainer? Eve? I mean, didn't a man write all of her lines?

HOMOPHOBIA: FEAR OF SAMENESS

Real men, like you, come first: their wants being their real
women, real women being shadows of their wants.

Your two palms pressed to her two palms? *Fine.* Your two lips
pressed to her two lips? *Fine.* One tulip nestled between

two petals of limb in the way one interprets a Georgia O'Keeffe?
Beautiful work of art. And two tulips lying side by side?

Doubly beautiful, so long as you're in the room, and the lights
are low, and your hand strokes of genius, the moonlight

catching that silver tongue in glory as you laugh. And this
is how you God, but forbid yourself that you didn't exist

in that space, that their hair was cut shorter than yours and
their lumberjack boots tracked mud onto the silk sheets.

Forbid they had full beards that even you, Almighty,
couldn't grow, that their voices came deep from the kegs

of their hairy bellies, that they're even larger than the law
you've laid into the bodies of who knows how many

girls going back to your fraternity days. You hate
to be challenged. You are a jealous type. You leak salt

from where love should come. And why? Because some liquors
are clear like water is and your old man disappeared into his

right fist and was never seen again. A man's greatest weapon
is his body, built with a gun attached—but if he's allowed it

to be matched, or removed at leisure, he can no longer hold
his hostages; his throne, then, is nothing more than a toilet.

I THINK I KNOW ONE WHEN I SEE ONE

In the mirror, admiring those pretty-ass eyebrows—
arched to perfection, enviable in terms of thickness,

their condition nice enough to inspire somebody's
asking whether by choice or not, if deliberately

done, maybe tweezed or waxed, because they
are just *too* fine. Flawless. Raised, but in a way

that raises suspicions as to whether the pictures
in his bedroom hang crooked because of some

eccentric taste. But they, in fact, are what he was
born with, among other things, such as a penis that

runs warm at night or eyes like hurricane spindles,
that study how men stand like obelisks of rock salt,

how some of them stride as if their legs are separated
by a big inconvenience, how every now and then their

faces fold over perfectly on the hinges of their noses.
But the men are not looking his way to know they are

being looked at, to misinterpret the gaze, to shape
their own brows, at once, both skeptical and scared

of something between them, perhaps an opposite
charge, feared so much so he utters, if not spits,

some flagrant word that must be struck down to
protect reputation: *hell naw, I ain't no damn fa...*

because that's truth in the raw, because if he had
been one, stomping about these streets, he might

already be on fire. Flamed by the fellas, in flames,
instead of in this bathroom with unflattering light,

trimmer hot in hand, revising his hairline a line
across the brow, booty call due soon to set him

straight.

WORKING DEFINITION OF A PREFIX: TRANS-

meaning, as applied to a human being:

Through   birth & rebirth
Through   yin & yang
Through   lie & its long black shadow

Through   the insult of puberty
Through   an inside joke
Through   the garment of a name

Through   the rainbow & its sour Skittles
Through   skin color & across

Across   a cross-
          section of socially ill cognitions

Through   pronouns
Through   some awkward sex
Through   stitches, in the sense of laughter splitting a seam along the jaw
Through   confetti

Across   the dance floor with stumbling courage
       & a compliment to land on its wings

Through that good, good sex

Through   the front door & out the back, in one motion

Through   both me & you, like an instrument of crime
                we've committed to their bodies & against

Through   being seen   through   across   the board,
                                a broad spectrum of bully & bullshit

    Through   truth & its long black shadow
    Through   yang & yin
    Through   death & death again

            & beyond   & beyond   & across the face—

a crescent of teeth, a blade of joy hard-fought for
            & the camera flashing & the body, electric with life.

AUTOPHOBIA: FEAR OF SELF

The history of red begins and ends with me, did you know?
Violence is the apple of my eye, its skin winking in the light like

a triggered alarm. I sleep with a cannon in my hand. My belly is
full of lead; my upset stomach is settled by bullets, awaiting spark

to spit up. A gun muzzle in the mouth, whether mine or yours,
leaves just enough space between chapped lips to hold a hymn

note: hallelujah. Read your Bible. I'm Cain as much as I'm Abel.
I'm an angel, sometimes. I'm all three of them at once: a trinity

or a triangular symbol of potentiality, of mathematical change.
I can't count the number of brothers I could be done in by, that

I could do in myself, if only I speak what I know—the boy would
be finished for all intents and purposes: a name, a vapor. But we'd

have our mamas' colors in common, always; the whispers would
travel pews like plates of small bills and coins, crown them unholy

messes of motherhood, but nobody truly knows what happened
back in that garden so many translations ago, if the apple in those

verses is in my eyes because it was in hers first, if it's metaphor
for a swollen *appetite*. Blame sugar, I guess; blame what's sweet

enough to damn. Diabetes runs in my family: what does it make
of the space between bodies canvased by shadow? I hear it draws

closed: boys lock eyes, stab each other in the dark, scream out for
their very souls. I can see it, like I see the choir director walking

by me. She calls him *sweet*; I think *no homo* and laugh where only
God hears me judge. I take to water and wade with my face down.

KATRINA

A wet dream is supposed to be
how wet precisely?

Around my ankles, a puddle
of love, rippling when I call her name.

Maybe this is when imagination
has gone too far, though it keeps
kissing its way toward the waist.

One body overruns another
with an appetite for liquid.

There's not a stroke that can save this
black boy barely buoyant, trying to get
on top of all the motion. Wondering: *how*
many Negroes she done made new just like this?

I count them, the fish in her sea,
from the inside. Mad dudes. Girls, too.
Old and young. But, my God, I want to
be alone in all of this. Drowning
in her. Gasping for a reason to stop.

Heard from again only once
the bubbles rise to the surface and pop—

my ecstasy exposed as three
syllables conjuring her on the tip
of my sharp breathing:

TJ's older sister, a senior,
wavy haired, with water's sway
when she walks, and if he caught
you looking, he'd kill you.

I mean, if she didn't kill you first,
put that good-good on you. What fools
try to call on her for: *la petite mort.*
A little death. Yes. That's it—

she's everybody's little black death.

I WILL SHOW YOU FEAR IN A HANDFUL OF DUST

after T.S. Eliot

Doing the laundry, as I believe laundry has always been done,
practiced religiously, one piece of clothing pulled away from

all others and reassigned according to a scheme of color, or
maybe a schema; meanwhile, the hand moves from darkness

toward light, executing a law of separation, like words that
approximate *the presence of moon* or *the presence of sun,*

some vocabulary lesson left in the recesses of my mind as most
things elementary school and simply elementary. Even in cleaning

there is order: the manner in which certain items are kept pure
by the avoidance of mixture, maybe an idea carried over to, or

carried over from, how we built our greatest cities—this load of
people here, this load there, always add bleach here, and so on

and so on. We all know how the process goes, but when T.S. Eliot
wrote, "I will show you fear in a handful of dust," we didn't fathom

just how revolutionary it was because the spin cycle hadn't been
popularized, nor had cable news been invented, and every drop

of blood was hand scrubbed, and the number of people who came
out looking pink was kept to a rigid minimum, which is to say,

the woman I love, back then, would never have come to exist and
my own hands would have their work and their guilt cut in half;

I wouldn't be thinking about how many of my foremothers did
this exact labor so cruelly capturing their station in life as darks.

HYDROPHOBIA: FEAR OF WATER

Drink it for good health. Drink it for relief from the rabid
heat. Drink it plenty, but do not drink a body of it

equaling the weight of your own—imagine an ocean
on top of an ocean, how one drowns the other so only one

exists in the end; in the war between water and water,
there can only be a single survivor: the swallower.

Ask: *how much am I made of again?* Not enough. Remember
trying to learn the strokes of kinetic floatation, pushing

through the enemy only to discover there is more of him
where he came from, and that he came from all over,

surrounding you with an obvious defeat, the mercy
of a nearby boundary between wet and dry all there was

to prevent the certain sinking feet deep into a not-ground,
but like fine soil, still a darkness. Even baptismal water is

a mild threat; more than sin lives in a river, and the salt licks
from the last great campaign for the right to air are fresh still.

And do well to remember that time itself is an ocean, too,
and that black body of yours, most of its weight, is ocean to

an ant, as are the cups of water you poured on an entire colony;
do remember how they tried to survive the flood but were

completely overwhelmed. In the marrow of your bones, this is
trigger: in your legs, two fibulas like banshee screams—long but

smothered thin whether from he or she tossed overboard—locked
still, unfit to kick resistance to the genocide of a color, a humankind.

"…EVERYDAY SOMETHING HAS TRIED TO KILL ME AND HAS FAILED"

after Lucille Clifton

What might do me in is the telling of a white lie.
Having my gut confused for a knife block.
The structural failure of my body to process sugar.

The ferry could capsize and my lungs will sponge the river
of its acids. Maybe hipsters have moved into this neighborhood,
made it safe, as danger always begins, or I've breathed
in the legacy of industry for too many years,
to the point this economy of blood must collapse.

There's the one of many silver bullets that could
take a chance at love and kiss my forehead, the chance
I'm taken for someone with a different name.

Maybe the next great war will pass me on the street and
claim me as a souvenir. I could be seen as a common criminal
and they decide to skip the trial completely; I could conjure
the beast that gnaws my bones just by being colorful.

Jumped, as a kind of broom into new beginnings—
yes, I can fathom that, too.

Cars can drive the speed limit or above. The body,
which is mostly water, likewise conducts electricity;

a Taser can be reached for and come up the trigger that
ends it all, and that's not just a movie the critics clap for.

The catcalling hard hats can miss hammering a nail,
leave a screw loose that would've helped bear the load
of light I will lose when it all comes down on me
like an answered prayer with booming thunder and a bolt.

In a moment of panic, I may forget the words needed to barter
for my life; there's the issue of a paycheck being taken away
at will, me being forced to eat myself to the point of invisibility
except for 32 teeth spread in the dust, ivory of easy poaching.

Planes crash to earth like the rare shooting star. Cells
multiply themselves and build jails on top of dwindling bone.
They can mount their flag in my eye for all I know, but
all I know is that they haven't yet: call it Jesus or dumb luck.

THE MELANCHOLIA

I've been known to walk through walls—with a door, through it,
juggling knives   without handles, my lifelines all
the deeper, as if traced back and forth in red ink on my palms.
And I'm a loaded rifle with a light trigger,   my penis some

redundant device tucked away into cotton drawers. An animal
is proven by the smell of me;   every tooth in my mouth is
a triangle with one angle below freezing, perfect for piercing
flesh—but I make sure to wear my muzzle.   I make sure

to swallow when the ache splits me: my head is a bottle of Aspirin
with one solitary pill inside, rattling around   like a marble.
I've been drinking more and more water. I still can't swim.
There is only   down. And somehow, I'm the socket and

the scissors in the same: an accidental harm, like a slip-Freudian.
Their words fly through the window of my mouth like   paper
airplanes into a darkening confusion. The howling wind blows me
fist-like, my bones like xylophone bars, but   as I lay sleep

nothing is heard from me except an acclaimed imitation of death.
I haven't remembered a dream in five years,   but I do know
in the back of my throat a man hangs by his neck, swaying when
I speak; I know that,   like a ghost, I walk through walls.

WATER COOLER TALK ENDING WITH THE COLORS OF AN AMERICAN FLAG

for Rafael Ramos and Wenjian Liu

They were quite simply assassinated – targeted for their uniform...
–WILLIAM BRATTON, NYPD COMMISIONER

Gun to my head, if you asked me what a bad cop looks like,
I'd say a *thug*.   You'd clap back: *what does a thug look like?*

Then I'd turn tables, like what play "thug music": *what
comes to mind for you?*—because I'd bet, if we engaged in this
Corporate American taboo, what you'd call *a thug*, I'd call
a cousin, and what my cousin would call *a pig*,   you'd call
a pulled pork sandwich. And on lunch break, we'd talk about how

black people (mostly men like me) don't smile in their pictures,
each one taken a mug shot on reserve starting as far back
as age thirteen, maybe younger.   Probably.

Truth is, I've rarely seen police officers (mostly the men) smile
in their pictures, either; this, seeing the world from opposite sides.
Eye-to-eye-to-eye: a single firearm drawn between two bodies
when lightning strikes,   and just that suddenly,

the sweetness of roses. A stone where the bones of a black person,
of a white person, sleep.   In our minds, not the Latino,
not the Asian man on lunch break, eating sandwiches in their cruiser,

dressed in uniform color of what we've said for so long
suppresses the brightness of colors like they were to the bone,
their pictures printed in all the newspapers, all over
the TV screen,   neither one of them smiling.

If I could ask them *why*? I believe they'd tell me, very sweetly,
it's not because of what they saw before, but what they saw coming.
Not the gun to their heads, but the gun   to mine, to yours.
In the end, we're all killed for who we are. When we are. Where:
assassinated all the same. Our blood the same, blue before it was red,
or white, or brown, or yellow, or black,   black,   black.

UNMAKING A FIST

after Naomi Shihab Nye

The push comes first, the disregard written in a thin brook of
alcohol from his chin to the floor. Then there's a voice deep

        inside saying an open hand is the diaspora of a fist, telling
        me *come home*, but I'm not a thug above most things, if

above anything at all. Please understand I'm not saying that I'm
better than a starving gut, that there aren't things I want, need

        but can't afford, that I don't have the electric rage of Watts
        I somehow can't explain besides the fact a moon is absent

from the midnight sky of my body. And truth be told, I'm no better
than the rope that started this, but my mother raised me right. My

        father raised me right. My grandmother and grandfather raised
        me right. That's four right turns right there, friend: always been

a square, but I still have sharp edges, corners of my own define
I can put claim to. I still have the threat of my skin to back me up,

        the color of everything that has burned to the ground, simplified
        to ash and cinder. Yes, maybe he has this, too. It doesn't matter,

really. I can either put up my dukes and free jazz or let the static,
let the electricity slide so we can both go home dancing without a

blemish on our shirts. And I make my choice, wave the flag within
like there's a cross painted on it I must represent, but there may

no be difference in the end. A fight found me tonight, regardless
of what I had planned with my peoples: picked some Skittles off

me that I walked four miles back and forth for in the rain. Make no
mistake, I know what I look like. I'm not in a position to say a bullet

doesn't already have my name on it. This is what it is to be prey to an
animal larger than you, to be in its belly from the moment you're born.

HOW DO YOU FORGIVE?

Don't squeeze. Ease up on the trigger. Reopen your
mouth. Remove the barrel. Mouth the deeper wound
with the wound called a mouth. Don't wound whoever
is near enough to hear you shatter into tears, sweat,
blood, scrap metal. Unload the clip, bullet by bullet,
until all of them are accounted for, definitively cold.
Disassemble the assault rifle. Take shots of liquor
to the chest in rapid fire. Set your heart on fire like
a straw man. Have a small change of heart. Find an
arrhythmia in the pulse of wrath. Box the shadows
and phantoms with a flashlight. Unclench your heart-
sized fist. Extend your open hand, palm up, like
an ironed-flat white flag. Politely wave off their
apology with your dominant hand. Twist a dishrag
like a chicken neck with your bare hands. Clean
the house until you can't fathom anything except
the color of water. Think clearly. Think within the
marrow of God. Bow and bend toward sources of
soft light. Be carried lightly inside the womb of a
love song. Love something better than you are.
Realize it's better to be alone than not be at all. Be
bigger than the many, many things that try to kill you
dead. Hang pictures of the dead on the wall, though
sometimes they harmed you in their practice of love.
Wall off certain rooms in the house, but let the house
stand. Save stomach for bread's breaking. Eat birds

because you believe in becoming what you consume,
how the saying goes, more easily through the mind than
even fresh air. Believe in a heaven up there equally, if not
more, than hell. Remember all the hell you went through
in order to survive. Survive, and don't tell them *sorry*.

ODE TO BLACK LOVE

Much threat to somebodies, sometimes you've been a fist.
Even more times a throwing of hands into the air, a shout
in the Holy Spirit from kinfolk as the broom is skipped,
all of them gathered in halo to witness what already is—
what you already are—replicate, and what you are is real
country-like: a ham hock stewing in a pot of collard greens,
butterbean, cheese grits kind of tender touching of insides,
a handmade ointment for braille backs and dog bites and
knots on the forehead from a nightstick, that's what you be,
that thick oil sheen force field surrounding a 'fro picked like
black cotton into a puff as if blunt smoke, what once graced
pages of *Ebony Magazine* in the heydays. You be so young
and so old at the same damn time. Back when their lips
sowed conspiracy in the fields, when they made a family
against orders, when a kid was made and only half theirs,
you were and were so fully, not lacking weight despite the
slimmer pickings of meat. Fully light, you were. Harlem's
lights, you were. The kiss of band's brass against the dark
pupil of history: found you blowing the hell out of a body
out of a saxophone, the roof off the house party, and when
they came in the still of night to set your roof on fire, call
you nigger as if the word could even own you, you didn't
tremble, said a gun ain't nothing next to God, and that's
why you always been my nigga fo' real fo' real. And for
the times when you dared a fool to and it came to blows,
because you were hard enough, because you were soft

enough that everybody came and went back home. See, you ain't anybody's bullet and never have been, but you're blood, like Jesus was blood, kind of Crip when you had and have to be, a pact between brothers without signs or colors, just daps and pounds, that's what you are. And not dead. And not dead. And not dead. And not a deadbeat, neither. Always been here, been the moles in her face and the hitch in his back, a watermelon without guilt split seven-some-odd ways un-sinfully. Matter of fact: a messiah—a messiah made of me and he and she. That's what you've been and be. What our mamas and daddies made, some old deep-fried recipe.

IN THEORY, WE ARE ALL HUMAN

Not a simple thing, no. Not to be taken lightly. To be
understood, and I do, that is, get the theory of you:
integral of human possibilities. The theory of your body
as a familiar machine, like mine, like something that
hums while it works a skin together where there had
been a rip before. The theory of skin, of its color
and discolor. The theory of your blood and bones,
like mine; your eyes and lashes, like mine; your nose;
your mouth, full of ocean, like mine. The theory
of freedom, which I take to be a naked feather,
dancing, almost like a hammock, back and forth, back
and forth in the passing wind. The theory of God
as asymptote and the theory of love as limit, the two,
tied together inside my head by a math problem.
The theory of law as inequality instead of equation.
The theory of a wedding dress and the theory of
a wedding dress on fire. The theory of binding breasts
like pages of a book needing to be read. The theory
of birth as death sentence. The theory of life as illness.
The theory of male and the theory of female and
the theory of neither and yet, still, this body, like mine,
graphed on so many dimensions. The theory of choice,
like reaching for an apple instead of an orange. The theory
of sin, like reaching for an apple. The theory of ribs
as prison bars. The theory of homelessness among
family. The theory of children who claim you, likewise,

as a blessing. The theory of your smile. The theory
of a rainbow after the storm, like the gift of a perfect
bridge over troubled waters. The theory of your hand
touching mine, incidentally, in the closet of a single
moment. The theory that one of us, in that moment,
did not exist in our right mind. The theory of mind as
illness. The theory of choice, again, but for which of us
and what between? The theory of sex and sacred and
the hard, hard practice. The theory of you. The theory
of me. The theory of a good person and the truth of
a bad, though, in theory, I cannot say who or

                                        won't.